Bears

Childrens Book About Bears

Terry Mason

Disclaimer

All rights reserved. No part of this e-book may be reproduced or transmitted in any form or by any means, electronic or mechanical, including photocopying, recording, or by any information storage and retrieval system, without the expressed written permission from the author and publishing company.

About Bears

Bears are Shy Too

Bears may look scary and fierce because of their huge size but they are more than that. Bears are actually quiet and solitary animals. That means they are often seen living alone. They are smart creatures. In presence of other creatures, they are shy and they can be great in hiding themselves.

Bears belong to the group of animals called mammals. Mammals are warm-blooded animals that give milk, give birth to, and feed their babies, and have hair or fur. There are many types of bears, and they have different colors too. Bears can be found in almost every part of the world, but there are no bears in Australia and Antarctica. There are 8 species of bears: Black, Asiatic, Brown, Panda, Polar, Spectacled, Sun, and Sloth.

Brown Bear Welcomes

Sleeping Time for Bears

Hibernation is the time during which animals experience low body temperature and they sleep for a very long time. This happens in winter time. Hibernators occasionally wake up from their sleep to get food and then they sleep again.

Bears are hibernators but they are different from other hibernators such as squirrels and skunks. Bears can sleep for as long as 7 months without drinking or eating. Bears usually have 40 to 50 heartbeats per minute but during hibernation, their heartbeats drop down to 8 beats per minute. Female bears sometimes give birth to cubs during hibernation. Only bears from cold places experiencing winter time hibernate. Asiatic bears living in warm places do not need to hibernate.

Bears and their Meal Time

Bears are omnivores. Omnivores are animals that eat both plants and meat. Humans are omnivores too.

To get food, bears hunt in the forest, or even rummage through garbage cans, for food. In the forest, animals such as the elk, caribou, and baby deer are what bears hunt for food. Bears living near a river hunt for fish.
As scavengers, bears also dig in garbage cans to look for food. Bears also look for nuts and berries for food. Panda bears mainly eat bamboo. Cubs or baby bears depend on their mothers for food. Mother bears feed their cubs their milk during the first year of life.

Brown Bear Fishing

Bears and Their Senses

Bears have excellent sense of smell, sense of hearing, and sense of sight. From plenty of miles away, bears can already smell not just food but also cubs and mates. Bears use their droppings and urine to mark their territory. In that way, other bears can smell if they are already crossing another bear's territory.

Bears use their eyesight remarkably to determine if the fruit they are eating is ripe or rotten. They use their keen sense of hearing to track and hunt for small animals and insects from the trees and bushes. These senses keep the bears alive and surviving.

Sitting Bear

Bears and the Mating Season

At the ages of 3 until 8 years, female bears can already mate with male bears to give birth to cubs. However, it depends on a female's weight and health if she can give birth.

The mating season begins in spring. Female bears and male bears begin living together to find their mates. Finding a mate and mating is not that simple for bears.

At first, female bears are afraid of the male bears because male bears are much larger than them. In order for a male to get close to a female, the male needs to earn the trust of the female. The male bear will follow a female bear from a distance until the female warms up to the male and eventually allows the male to get closer to her. That's how bears find their mates.

Bear Cubs

Female bears give birth to cubs during the winter, the time of their hibernation. When born, cubs seem like helpless creatures. They cannot hear, see, and even feed because they don't have teeth yet. Mothers take care of their cubs.

Bear cubs are playful, especially after hibernation when they are high on energy and are bigger. A mother bear allows her cubs to play-fight and when things get rough enough, the mother bear will swat her cubs to discipline them.

Cubs will remain with their mothers for about a year. Some stay with their mothers until 2 years of age.

How Bears Walk

Most animals walk on their toes. Bears, on the other hand, are like humans when they walk—flat-footed. Walking on flat feet allows bears to walk upright. Giant pandas, however, do not have heel pads. This makes walking flat difficult so giant pandas walk on their toes more often.

Aside from flat feet, bears have sharp and long claws on their paws. Their claws are shorter on their back paws. They use their longer claws on their front paws when climbing.

Polar bears have special feet. They have webbed toes. They use their webbed feet for swimming and walking in the snow.

Syrian Brown Bear

Predators and Species

When it comes to being predators or prey, bears are more like the predators most of the time. Being huge in size and fierce when angered, bears appear very intimidating and scary to other animals. The only threats faced by bears are other bears and humans.

On the other hand, things are not the same with small female bears and cubs. Other large animals may attack small cubs especially if the mother bear is away. Even large male bears attack cubs and small female bears for food. That is one reason why female bears do not want male bears to get close to them at first during mating season.

Bears defend themselves by making themselves look bigger. They do this by standing up on their hind legs and then fluffing up their fur. They may growl and they may pound on the ground when they are angry. It may not be necessary for bears to attack because other creatures may have gone away. Mother bears, however, may choose to attack to protect their cubs.

Bear fight

Asiatic Bear

Asiatic Bears can be found in East Asia, in the tropical mountainous regions of Malaysia, China, Cambodia, Afghanistan, India, and Taiwan. Asiatic bears are also called as Tibetan black bear, Himalayan black bear, and Moon bear.

Asiatic bears have black fur with a cream colored Y-shaped line on the chest. Their ears are large and they have long and fluffy hair around the neck. Compared with other species, this bear species is fiercer.

Bears are losing their habitat due to increasing human population and creation of more farmlands. Because of this, the bears hunt even domestic and farm animals for food. This puts them in danger because humans are ready to shoot when they see the bears on their land.

Asiatic Black Bear

Black Bear

Black bears are not necessarily black in color. There are bears belonging to the species of black bears but their furs are in brown, gray, and cream. Most black bears are black in color but there are some in different colors. Black bears are found in the tundra of Alaska and Canada and in the forests of Mexico and Central America.

The eyes of black bears are small. Their noses are long and their ears are rounded. Their tails are shorter compared to those of other species. Black bears are medium-sized bears just like Asiatic bears.

There are 16 subspecies of black bears; 8 of them can be found in British Columbia in Canada.

Black Bear

Brown Bear

Brown bears are seen in mountainous forests, meadows, and valleys of Canada, the Central USA, Europe, and Asia.

There is one characteristic of bears that makes them recognized as brown bears: their shoulder humps. Brown bears have strong shoulders for digging up roots and tearing logs apart for food hunting. Brown bears have the ability to move logs and rocks and to dig through the hard ground by using the strength of their shoulder muscles and their long and sharp claws.

Brown bears make their own dens. The den often looks like a tunnel going down into a small room where they hibernate. The female brown bear will sleep all throughout the winter. Female brown bears can even give birth while sleeping, never waking up during the birth of their cubs.

Brown Bear on Alaska fishing

Giant Panda

The giant panda, compared to other kinds of bears, is unique. This cute and cuddly, black and white panda is a favorite of many. It has big, black eyes. Pandas are excellent climbers. They can also swim to escape when they feel any sign of danger.

Only found in China, giant pandas are also considered endangered species. That means that there remains very few of them today. Only around 1000 pandas remain alive today because of the increasing human population. Some people have even hunted pandas for their fur.

Female panda bears usually give birth to one or two pandas at a time. When a female panda gives birth to two or more panda cubs, the mother will only take care of one of them. The others will soon die.

Polar Bear

Considered to be the world's largest predators on land, polar bears are found in the Arctic, Alaska, Denmark, Canada, and Norway. At present, the Arctic serves as the habitat of about 40,000 polar bears.

During hibernation, female polar bears dig their caves in a snow drift and they stay there all throughout the winter. They come out after the winter together with their cubs.

Although polar bears are large animals, polar bear cubs are as tiny as rats when they are born. They become as big as humans at one year of age.

White-Polar-Bear

Sloth Bear

The sloth bear and the sloth are two different animals although the two have similar characteristics. Sloth bears, like sloths, hang from branches, carry cubs on their backs, and live near other sloth bears. Father sloth bears even help with the mother sloth bears to take care and raise their babies. Sloths are very slow animals. Sloth bears, however, are not.

Sloth bears have lips that are hairless unlike other kinds of bears. They also have gaps between teeth and their tongues are long. Sloth bears eat termites, insects, eggs, carrion, and honeycombs.

Sloth bears can be found living in the grasslands and evergreen forests of Bangladesh, Burma, Nepal, Sri Lanka, and India.

Indian Sloth Bear

Spectacled Bear

Spectacled bears, also commonly referred to as Andean bears, can be found living in the Andes Mountains. The spectacled bears are named as such because they appear as if they are wearing spectacles. This is because of the markings they have on their faces.

Spectacled bears, also commonly referred to as Andean bears, can be found living in the Andes Mountains. The spectacled bears are named as such because they appear as if they are wearing spectacles. This is because of the markings they have on their faces.

Sun Bear

A small bear, the sun bear is also known as the Malayan sun bear and as the honey bear. Sun bears have short, black fur and yellow-orange fur in the shape of a horseshoe on the chest. This shape symbolizes the rising sun, as many believe it to be.

Sun bears eat birds, lizards, rodents, honey, and termites. They also have long and sharp claws which they use for tearing trees open. Sun bears live in places with a tropical climate. That means they do not need to hibernate. Sun bears are commonly seen in Southeast Asia.

Grizzly Bear

Grizzly bears are a subspecies of brown bears. Grizzly bears have the characteristic shoulder humps of brown bears. They have concave faces and their claws are long. They have a dark brown color but some are colored light black and some are dark.

Their long hair around the neck has tints of white, making them appear grizzly. That is the main reason why this bear is called a Grizzly bear.

Grizzly bears eat caribou, moose, and elk but they also feed on grass, roots, insects, fish, carrion, and other small mammals.

Brown-Bear-grizzly-bear

Bear Mythology and Folklore

.Pandas are considered to be "National Treasures" in China.

•In the First Nations or Native American culture, the bears are the dream-keepers because of their hibernation. They are also referred to as the keepers of medicines.

•In British Columbia and near Alaska, the Kermode bear is believed to have mystical powers.

•The legend of First Nations says that Kermode bears were once white in color to remind people of the Ice Age.

•The Greek legend tells the story of the Big Dipper, the Ursa Major constellation. The god Zeus fell in love with Callisto, giving her a son named Arcas. Zeus' wife Hera was jealous so she turned Callisto into a bear. When the grown-up Arcas was hunting, he went against a bear, not knowing that the bear was his own mother. In fear that Callisto might die, Zeus placed Callisto into the night sky as the constellation the Big Dipper, or Ursa Major.

•The Vikings and the Celts admire and revere the strength and power of bears.

Fun Facts about Bears

- The bear with the shaggiest fur is the sloth bear.
- Bears have two layers of fur: a short layer of warmth and a long layer to keep water away.
- Bears can live up to 30 years.
- Polar bears are carnivores. The other kinds of bears are omnivores.
- Koala bears are marsupials and do not belong to the bear family.
- Bears can run up to a speed of 40 miles per hour.
- Bears can see colors.
- Polar bears can swim at a speed of 100 miles per hour.

Comprehension Questions

1. What kind of bears have shoulder humps?
2. Do all black bears have black fur?
3. What kind of bear is a Grizzly Bear?
4. What type of animals are bears: herbivore, carnivore, or omnivore?
5. What type of bear has webbed toes?
6. Is the sloth the same as a sloth bear?
7. During what season do bears hibernate?
8. What is the largest land predator?
9. What species of bear is considered to be China's national treasure?
10. For how many years can a bear live?

Answer Comprehension Questions

1. Brown Bears

2. No. Some are brown, gray, and cream in color.

3. Brown Bear

4. Omnivore. They eat both plants and meat. The only exception is the polar bear which is a carnivore.

5. Polar bear

6. No. They are two different animals.

7. Winter

8. Polar bear

9. Giant panda

10. 30 years

Made in the USA
Lexington, KY
27 November 2018